FAMOUS MOVIE MONSTERS™

INTRODUCING

FRANKENSTEIN MEETS THE WOLF MAN

The Rosen Publishing Group, Inc.,
New York

GREG ROZA

For Lincoln

Published in 2007 by The Rosen Publishing Group, Inc.
29 East 21st Street, New York, NY 10010

Library of Congress Cataloging-in-Publication Data

Roza, Greg.
Introducing Frankenstein meets the Wolf Man/Greg Roza.
    p. cm.—(Famous movie monsters)
Filmography: p.
Includes bibliographical references and index.
ISBN 1-4042-0825-9 (library binding:alk. paper)
1. Frankenstein meets the Wolf Man (Motion picture) I. Title:
Frankenstein meets the Wolf Man. II. Title. III. Series.
PN1997.F685R69 2006
791.43'72—dc22

2005034038

Manufactured in Malaysia

On the cover: Frankenstein's monster (Bela Lugosi) grapples with the Wolf Man (Lon Chaney Jr.).

CONTENTS

CHAPTER 1

FRANKENSTEIN MEETS THE WOLF MAN

Mist swirls over the ground in a graveyard in Llanwelly Village, Wales. Two silent figures approach a tomb marked by the family name "Talbot." The grave robbers climb into the tomb through an opening above the door.

The cobweb-draped tomb holds the remains of members of the Talbot family. The grave robbers locate the coffin they have come to find. Hoping to find riches that were reportedly buried with Lawrence Talbot, the men pry the heavy slab off the top of the coffin.

It appears as though Talbot has not decayed over the four years that he has lain there. The men begin searching the body for money, and one takes the ring from Talbot's finger. As light from the full moon filters into the dark chamber, the hand of the late Lawrence Talbot begins to rise! It grasps the arm of the man who has just removed the ring. The other man flees the tomb, despite the cries for help from his partner in crime. It seems that Talbot, who once terrorized the village as the Wolf Man, is not dead after all.

Two grave robbers look on in horror as Lawrence Talbot (Lon Chaney Jr.) raises his hand from his coffin in the opening scene of *Frankenstein Meets the Wolf Man*. This scene—complete with a fog-shrouded cemetery, a full moon behind drifting clouds, and a dark tomb filled with cobwebs—creates the perfect mood for the monster story that follows.

After killing the grave robber, the Wolf Man roams the streets of nearby Cardiff until he collapses and changes back into human form. Lying unconscious on a side street, Talbot is found by a policeman. He is taken to a hospital, where he becomes the patient of Dr. Frank Mannering.

Talbot tries in vain to convince the doctor and a detective that he is a werewolf. He wants nothing more than to die and put an end to the curse that makes him transform into a werewolf. Unfortunately, no one will believe his fantastic stories. That night, Talbot changes into the Wolf Man once again and roams through the town of Cardiff, killing a policeman.

The next morning, Talbot awakens in the hospital, with no memory of what transpired the night before. While Mannering and the local chief of police investigate Talbot's past, Talbot escapes from the hospital. He travels in search of an old gypsy woman he once knew named Maleva, whom he hopes can help him. Years ago, Talbot was bitten by a werewolf. He killed the werewolf, but it was too late—once bitten, he was doomed to transform into a werewolf himself.

Maleva is the mother of the werewolf whom Talbot killed. When Talbot finds her, he begs her to help him end the curse and allow him to die. She reluctantly agrees to help. There is only one man who can help him, she tells him—Dr. Frankenstein.

Talbot and Maleva travel to Vasaria, Germany, in search of Dr. Frankenstein, the mad scientist who once tried to create a living being from dead body parts. After inquiring about the doctor's whereabouts in a small tavern, they are informed that the doctor and his hideous monster are dead, and that his castle lies in ruins. Talbot is crushed, fearing that he is doomed to live eternally as a bloodthirsty werewolf.

That very night, there is a full moon. Knowing that he may harm her, Talbot flees from Maleva. He transforms into a werewolf. Unable to control himself, the Wolf Man murders the young daughter of the tavern owner. The villagers, terrified that Frankenstein's monster has returned, form an angry mob. Armed with torches and farm implements, they go in search of the monster. They see the Wolf Man, who they mistake for Frankenstein's monster. As the Wolf Man flees the angry mob, he suddenly plunges through an old cellar door and into the abandoned, underground ruins of Dr. Frankenstein's laboratory. Knocked unconscious by the fall, he transforms back into Lawrence Talbot.

When Talbot awakens, he searches his surroundings and discovers Frankenstein's monster frozen in a block of ice. Talbot thaws the monster out and convinces him to help find Dr. Frankenstein's secret diary. They are not able to find it, but Talbot realizes that the late doctor's laboratory must hold the key to ending the curse of the werewolf.

Disguised as a man named Taylor—a real estate buyer interested in purchasing the Frankenstein estate—Talbot meets with Elsa Frankenstein, the late Dr. Frankenstein's daughter. Talbot and Elsa are invited to a town festival that night by the mayor of Vasaria. Dr. Mannering shows up unexpectedly, and Talbot explains to Mannering that he is searching for the diary of Dr. Frankenstein to discover a way to die and put an end to the curse. Suddenly, Frankenstein's monster arrives. He is looking for Talbot, the only person who he can consider a friend. Escaping the angry and terrified townspeople together, Talbot and the monster flee back to the ruins of the castle.

Mannering and Elsa decide to team up to help end the suffering of both creatures. They convince the people of Vasaria that they will once and for all rid the land of the monsters. Elsa allows Mannering to use her father's secret diary to plan for the procedure. Mannering discovers a way to take the life energy from Talbot, thus ending his life and the curse of the werewolf. He also decides to do the same thing to Frankenstein's monster.

Mannering restores Dr. Frankenstein's laboratory to working order. Unable to contain his excitement for experimenting with life and death, Mannering straps both Talbot and the monster to tables and attaches wires to their heads. Although he originally planned to use the equipment to sap their life energy and end their suffering, Mannering has become obsessed with the monsters. He cannot bring himself to destroy Frankenstein's creation. Instead, he decides that he must find out what happens when the life forces of both monsters are maximized. Instead of sapping their life force, he reverses the electrical current and gives both monsters full strength! At the same time, the light of the full moon enters the laboratory through a high window. Mayhem ensues. While the others flee to safety, both monsters break free of their bonds and begin to battle in the underground laboratory. They hurl scientific equipment at each other to the sounds of explosions and horrific growls. While the monsters battle on, the father of the little girl whom

In their first scene together, Lawrence Talbot releases Frankenstein's monster (Bela Lugosi) from its frozen ice tomb located beneath the ruins of Dr. Frankenstein's castle. The monster, wearing its trademark black blazer, leads Talbot on a search for Dr. Frankenstein's secret journal. Talbot hopes to use the doctor's scientific notes about life and death to rid himself of the curse of the werewolf.

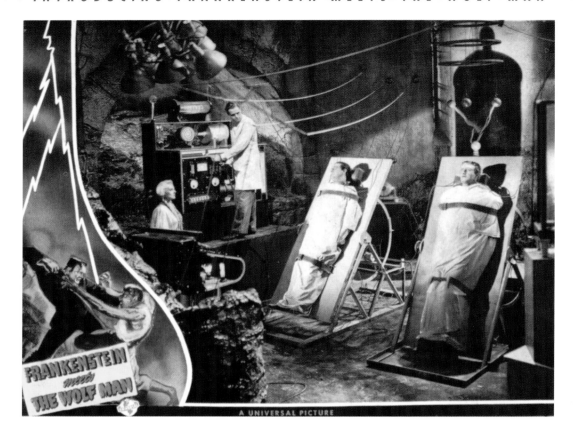

This colorized advertisement for *Frankenstein Meets the Wolf Man* shows one of the movie's final scenes. Talbot and Frankenstein's monster are strapped to tables and connected to Dr. Frankenstein's scientific machinery. Dr. Mannering (Patric Knowles) is operating the machines while the Baroness Elsa Frankenstein (Ilona Massey) watches.

the Wolf Man killed climbs up to a dam overlooking the castle. He plants dynamite on the dam, planning to destroy the castle and everything it contains. As the fight reaches a terrifying peak, the dam explodes, sending water rushing down over the castle. The monsters rage on as the torrent envelops them.

CHAPTER 2

HISTORY OF THE MOVIE

The first motion pictures made in the 1890s were usually very short—sometimes only a half-minute long. People were entranced with the idea of moving images, and early movies were often very simple. However, it wasn't long before people were trying to film tales of adventure, drama, and even horror.

Most critics agree that the first horror movie was Thomas Edison's *Frankenstein* (1910). This movie lasted only sixteen minutes, but it terrified moviegoers. In 1919, the German psychological horror film *The Cabinet of Dr. Caligari* sparked a horror movie revolution in Europe and in the United States. This movie was followed by other silent horror and science fiction classics such as *Nosferatu* (1922), *Faust* (1926), and *Metropolis* (1926).

UNIVERSAL HORROR

Universal Studios created a series of highly popular monster movies between the 1920s

This still from the first Universal horror movie, *The Phantom of the Opera,* shows the phantom (Lon Chaney Sr.) seated at the organ in his underground hideout. A seasoned stage actor, Chaney insisted upon creating his own skeletal makeup effects for this character. Lon Chaney's portrayal of the mad, scarred musician terrified and fascinated moviegoers.

and the 1950s. Universal horror films popularized the "classic" movie monsters. The first Universal horror movie—*The Phantom of the Opera*—was released in 1925 before movies had sound. The movies *Dracula* and *Frankenstein*, both released in 1931, are considered by many to be the most entertaining and successful of the Universal horror movies. The other classic movie monsters immortalized by Universal horror films include the

Mummy, the Wolf Man, the Invisible Man, and the Creature from the Black Lagoon.

Many of the Universal horror films made during the 1930s are still popular with audiences all over the world today. By the early 1940s, however, Universal Studios no longer had the large budget it once had, partially because of the effects of World War II on the U.S. economy. As a result, the studio started releasing cheap sequels in the hope of capitalizing on its monster movie blockbusters.

In this advertisement, the beautiful Elsa Frankenstein watches helplessly as the monsters battle in the background. In the lower right, Maleva the gypsy (Maria Ouspenskaya) beckons to viewers with a mysterious and foreboding glare. *Frankenstein Meets the Wolf Man* was the first picture Universal made in which the two famous monsters did battle.

In the early 1940s, Universal Studios began making movies in which its movie monsters teamed up. These movies are sometimes called monster rallies because they are sequels to more than a single series of films. *Frankenstein Meets the Wolf Man*, for example, is a sequel to the four *Frankenstein* movies that came before it and to *The Wolf Man*. While most of these movies were not as popular as the Universal horror movies of the 1930s, they helped to sustain Universal's reputation with moviegoers. *Frankenstein Meets the Wolf Man* was the most successful monster rally movie.

BACK STORY

The story related in *Frankenstein Meets the Wolf Man* is the continuation of two storylines that had been established in previous Universal movies. The first of these storylines involves the creation and troubled existence of the Frankenstein monster.

The first of the *Frankenstein* movies was *Frankenstein* (1931), in which the mad doctor Henry Frankenstein creates a man from body parts and brings it to life. In *The Bride of Frankenstein* (1935), the monster forces Dr. Frankenstein to build him a mate. In *The Son of Frankenstein* (1939), Frankenstein's son, Wolf, is convinced by Ygor, an evil blacksmith played by Bela Lugosi, to wake his father's creation from a coma, and the terror begins anew. In the 1942 film *The Ghost of Frankenstein*, Ygor blackmails the second son of Frankenstein, Ludwig, into transplanting his own brain into the monster (played by Lon Chaney Jr.). The result is a monster more terrible than ever before.

Frankenstein Meets the Wolf Man also resumes the story that began with the movie *The Wolf Man*. In *The Wolf Man*, Lawrence Talbot (also played by Lon Chaney Jr.) tries to save a woman from the clutches of a gypsy fortune-teller who has turned into a werewolf (played by Bela Lugosi). Talbot kills the werewolf, but he is bitten in the process. The gypsy's mother, Maleva, informs Talbot that he is now a werewolf, too. At the next full moon, Talbot transforms into the Wolf Man and runs amok until he is slain by his own father.

THE MEN WHO PLAYED THE MONSTERS

Both monsters in *Frankenstein Meets the Wolf Man* were played by notable horror actors. Lon Chaney Jr.—son of silent film star Lon Chaney—played the role of the Wolf Man. Bela Lugosi played the role of Frankenstein's monster. This was not the first time that Chaney or Lugosi had played monsters in the movies.

BELA LUGOSI

Bela Lugosi (born Bela Ferenc Dezso Blasko) is best remembered for his portrayal of Dracula on stage and screen. A seasoned stage actor from Hungary, Lugosi was selected to play the famous vampire in the 1927 Broadway play *Dracula*, which had been adapted from the novel of the same name by Bram Stoker. The movie was, in turn, adapted from the 1931 theater production.

This portrait of a young Bela Lugosi shows the memorable horror movie actor without his makeup, something moviegoers rarely saw. Even without his monster makeup, Lugosi's piercing gaze reminds viewers of his chilling roles.

Playing the mysterious Count Dracula made Lugosi a superstar in the United States. Lugosi had passed on a chance to play Frankenstein's monster in 1931 because the role

Taken around 1932, this picture shows Lon Chaney Jr. before he became famous for his roles in Universal horror movies. At this time, Chaney was known by his birth name, Creighton Chaney.

offered him no lines and his face would have been hidden beneath heavy makeup. The part went to Lugosi's long-time movie-monster rival, Boris Karloff. As a result, he relished the chance to play the role of the monster in *Frankenstein Meets the Wolf Man*.

LON CHANEY JR.

Lon Chaney Jr. (born Creighton Tull Chaney) grew up watching his parents perform on stage and in movies. His father, Lon Chaney, was an actor who became famous for his many movie-monster roles, particularly his performance in the silent screen version of *The Phantom of the Opera*. Lon Chaney Jr. became a horror movie star with his memorable portrayal of Lawrence Talbot in the movie *The Wolf Man*.

Chaney reprised his role as Lawrence Talbot in 1943's *Frankenstein Meets the Wolf Man*. While Universal's other great monsters—Dracula, Frankenstein, and the Mummy—were played by a number of actors, Lon Chaney Jr. was the only actor to play the Wolf Man.

THE MEN WHO MADE THE MONSTERS

The man responsible for creating the monsters in *Frankenstein Meets the Wolf Man* was makeup artist Jack Pierce. Pierce had created all of Universal's classic horror monsters between 1931 and 1943. His most famous creation was that of Frankenstein's monster. Makeup sessions with Pierce were often long and difficult, and they usually required that the actors sit still for many hours. Although working with Pierce could be a grueling experience for actors, the results he achieved were nothing short of spectacular.

The special-effects cameraman who worked on *Frankenstein Meets the Wolf Man* was John P. Fulton. Fulton often used a special-effects technique called stop-motion photography. During this process, a cameraman takes a picture of an object, moves the object to a new position, and then takes another picture. This painstaking process is repeated many times, frame by frame. When the film is run through a projector, the object that was photographed appears to move.

To create the werewolf transformation scenes, Fulton first filmed Chaney without makeup. He then stopped the camera to allow Pierce to apply the first layer of makeup. After the first layer of makeup was applied, Fulton captured a few more seconds of film. Fulton and Pierce repeated this process until the transformation was complete.

Once all the segments were filmed, Fulton pieced them together to create the illusion of Talbot gradually turning into the Wolf Man. Pierce used glue and yak hair to create the effect

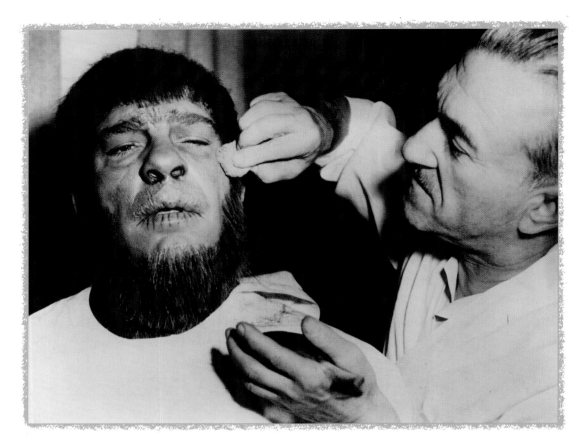

Universal makeup wizard Jack Pierce applies makeup to the face of Lon Chaney Jr. during filming of *Frankenstein Meets the Wolf Man*. Some reports say that Chaney and Pierce did not get along very well. Chaney disliked having to stay still for so many hours while Pierce—a self-proclaimed perfectionist—created one of the most recognized movie monsters of all time.

of Talbot's transformation, and the makeup was extremely uncomfortable. Although the on-screen transformation took only about ten seconds, the makeup session and photographic processes often took up to six hours. In fact, the original training session for this transformation is rumored to have lasted about eighteen hours.

STUNTS AND STUNTMEN

Lugosi and Chaney weren't the only performers to portray the monsters in *Frankenstein Meets the Wolf Man*. Two stuntmen also put on the makeup and appeared in the movie. Lugosi was fifty-eight years old at the time of filming and in poor health. He was so sick that he couldn't appear in all the scenes. Viewers can't help but notice that Frankenstein sometimes appears rather weak and nonthreatening (when played by Lugosi) and sometimes appears strong and quick (when played by stuntmen).

The first time the Frankenstein monster appears in *Frankenstein Meets the Wolf Man*, he is frozen behind a wall of ice. The camera moves in close for a shot of the monster's face. However, it is not Lugosi beneath the heavy makeup, but stuntman Gil Perkins. The reason for this substitution isn't completely clear. It may have been because of Lugosi's poor health, or because Lugosi wasn't on the set that day. Or it simply could have been because Lugosi, a notoriously difficult actor to work with, refused to cooperate with the director.

Stuntman Eddie Parker also played the role of Frankenstein's monster for the more active and strenuous parts. According to Universal horror film expert Donald F. Glut, Parker can be seen playing both monsters in the final battle, and Gil Perkins can be seen playing the Wolf Man for certain shots. The reasons for these changes are not known for sure, but it may have had to do with the availability of the actors and stuntmen, or the physical nature of the action. Parker was the taller of the two men, and he was used primarily for distant shots. Perkins played Frankenstein's monster for some close-ups.

CHAPTER 3

EVIL ORIGINS

Werewolves—sometimes called lycanthropes—have long been the subject of legends from a number of different cultures. Werewolf fables and other shape-shifting stories are found in ancient legends from all over the world. There is no single origin for the werewolf myths that we recognize today. Rather, these myths are a mixture of stories from different times and places.

Some werewolf myths describe people transforming completely into wolves, while some describe creatures that resemble wolflike men (much like Chaney's Wolf Man). Still other stories describe crazed humans acting in the manner of wild animals, particularly wolves. The werewolf that we are familiar with today is a combination of all of these legends.

KING LYCAON

Some of the oldest werewolf myths come from ancient Greece. Perhaps the most common story tells of a cruel and conceited king named Lycaon, who tried to deceive Zeus, the king of the gods, into eating human flesh.

This scene from *The Epic of Gilgamesh* was created by the Chaldean people of the Babylonian empire. Chaldean seals were created by carving a scene around a cylinder of stone. The stone was then rolled on wet clay, producing a flat picture. This detail shows Gilgamesh fighting a lion *(center)*, and Enkidu battling the Bull of Heaven *(right)*.

Zeus easily saw through Lycaon's trick. Some versions of the myth say that Zeus killed Lycaon and his fifty sons with bolts of lightning. Another version tells that Zeus transformed Lycaon into a wolf or a wolflike man. It is interesting to note that the term "lycanthropy"—the ability to undergo a transformation into a wolf—was originally derived from a combination of Lycaon's name (the Greek word *lykos* means "wolf") and the Greek word *anthropos*, which means "person."

THE EPIC OF GILGAMESH

Many historians believe that the Babylonian poem *The Epic of Gilgamesh* contains the first reference to a shape-shifting creature in literature. Written around 2000 BC, it is the oldest work of writing in the world. The story is about a king named Gilgamesh, who is two-thirds god and one-third human. Gilgamesh's people complain to the gods that he is a harsh leader, so the gods create a wolflike creature named Enkidu to battle Gilgamesh. Enkidu is a creature with long hair who protects wild animals from human hunters. Gilgamesh sends a priestess to tame Enkidu, who then transforms from a wild creature into a man.

GILLES GARNIER

Reports of werewolves became common in the sixteenth century, especially in France. The story of Gilles Garnier is one of the most famous examples of lycanthropy from this time period.

In 1573, Gilles Garnier, a hermit in the town of Dole, France, was convicted of making a pact with the devil. In the year before this trial, several children had been found brutally murdered. Some witnesses believed that a wild animal, most

VIKING BERSERKERS

Berserkers were Norse warriors who were known for fighting with furious abandon, attacking their enemies fearlessly and violently. Some berserkers went into battle wearing the skins of bears or wolves in order to frighten their opponents into thinking that they were wild animals. The word "berserker" comes from a Norse word that means "bear shirt." Many historians believe that this practice contributed to early werewolf legends in Europe.

likely a wolf, had killed the children. Others testified that Garnier had killed and even eaten them. These witnesses explained that Garnier was a scruffy individual with bushy eyebrows that met in the middle of his forehead. Some witnesses reported that Garnier transformed into a wolf before committing the horrible acts, while others claimed to have seen him attack people in human form.

This woodcut, titled "The Werewolf," was created around 1512 by a German artist named Lucas Cranach the Elder. Around this time in Europe, accusing criminals of being werewolves was common. These so-called werewolves—like Gilles Garnier and the one illustrated in this image—were thought to be possessed by the devil, and were usually put to death.

The court records indicate that Garnier was an evil person who killed and even ate children, but was he an actual werewolf? During his trial, Garnier confessed to the murders, claiming that he had made a deal with the devil. Garnier himself believed that he had transformed into a wolf when committing these crimes. As with most reports of lycanthropy, however, there is not enough evidence to prove it.

Today, lycanthropia is a real medical affliction that describes a person who thinks that he or she is capable of transforming into a wolf. Although they are often considered to

For four decades, Curt Siodmak *(right)* wrote and directed horror movies, many of which were big hits. Here, Siodmak holds the hand of actor Don Megowan between takes of the 1958 TV movie *Tales of Frankenstein.*

be the same thing, this medical terminology highlights the difference between lycanthropes and werewolves. A lycanthrope is generally considered a person with a mental illness; a werewolf is a creature of legend or myth.

UNIVERSAL WEREWOLVES

The Wolf Man and *Frankenstein Meets the Wolf Man* popularized several key myths regarding werewolves, including the notions that a person transforms into a werewolf when the moon is full, that werewolves can be killed by silver, and that werewolves are marked by the sign of the pentagram. While these ideas have appeared in various ancient myths, screenwriter Curt Siodmak combined them all to create a powerful mythology for the werewolves of Universal's horror movies. These concepts have been adopted by many subsequent werewolf movies.

FRANKENSTEIN'S MONSTER

Along with Dracula, Frankenstein's monster is perhaps the most well-known movie monster of all time. Today, most people picture Frankenstein's monster as an unintelligent, growling, lumbering beast with a fondness for mayhem. Many people are surprised to find that the original story of *Frankenstein* presents a creature that displays both intelligence and deeply human emotions. Many are equally surprised to learn that the original novel was written by a nineteen-year-old woman!

MARY WOLLSTONECRAFT SHELLEY

Mary Wollstonecraft Shelley was born in London, England, on August 30, 1797. During her life, Shelley was constantly surrounded by talented writers and their influence. Her father, William Godwin, and her mother, Mary Wollstonecraft, were both famous writers. Her husband, Percy Bysshe Shelley, is today considered one of the finest writers of the romantic period.

Mary Shelley wrote novels, poetry, short stories, essays, and travel journals, but none was as popular or enduring as her first novel—*Frankenstein*. Shelley is also known for her devotion to the editing and promotion of her late husband Percy Bysshe Shelley's writing. Thanks to Mary Shelley's work, Percy Shelley is known today as one of the greatest Romantic poets.

Mary Shelley was also constantly surrounded by sadness and tragedy. Her mother died shortly after giving birth to her. Although Shelley gave birth to four children, only one lived to adulthood. These two elements of Shelley's life—her contact with literary geniuses and her tragic experiences—would help her to create one of the most famous gothic novels of all time.

THE CONTEST

In 1816, when Shelley was just nineteen years old, she and her husband met the renowned English poet Lord Byron while vacationing in Geneva, Switzerland. The writers playfully engaged in a contest to see who could write the scariest ghost story. The winner was Shelley's most celebrated work of literature: *Frankenstein, or The Modern Prometheus*. Published anonymously in 1818, the novel became an instant best-seller, despite the fact that critics almost unanimously hated it. It both horrified and entertained readers, while at the same time making insightful observations about science, society, religion, and human emotions. In just five years, a second edition was printed, this time featuring Shelley's name on the cover. In the same year, the first of many stage adaptations was produced.

SHELLEY'S MONSTER

In Shelley's story, Dr. Victor Frankenstein, a young scientist who rejects many of the established scientific ideas of the time, discovers how to create life in dead tissue. He succeeds in creating a human being, but he is horrified by his creation and abandons it.

The two meet later in the story, and the monster explains his feelings to the doctor in surprisingly articulate language. The monster has been rejected by everyone, including his creator.

His feelings of abandonment and rejection led the monster to seek revenge against his creator by killing the doctor's youngest brother. The monster demands that the doctor create a partner for him. When the doctor fails to do this, the monster murders the doctor's best friend and fiancée. The story ends with Dr. Frankenstein chasing his creation to the Arctic Circle, where the doctor is rescued and the monster is presumed to be dead.

Shelley's monster is certainly a terrifying one, but he is not the mindlessly blood-thirsty one most people are familiar with today. Shelley's monster was deserted by his "father" and despised by society. These emotional ordeals left the monster bitter and alone, transforming his curiosity and confusion into malice and vengeance.

UNIVERSAL'S MONSTER

Since its creation in 1816, *Frankenstein* has had a great influence on popular culture. It is credited as being one of the most chilling gothic novels of all time, as well as the first work of science fiction. Shelley's work is still read and taught today. In addition to the literary world, *Frankenstein* has influenced many other areas of contemporary culture, from cartoons and comic books to toys and breakfast cereals.

Perhaps the most notable influence Shelley's story has had on modern society is in the movie industry. The first movie starring Frankenstein's monster, titled *Frankenstein*, was produced by Thomas Edison in 1910. Since this time, Frankenstein's monster has continued to be a popular topic in the realm of horror movies. It was Universal's movie *Frankenstein* (1931)

This still from the 1931 movie *Frankenstein* shows the cruel lab assistant Fritz (Dwight Frye) taunting the monster, played by Boris Karloff. Karloff was five feet eleven inches tall but he wore heavy, thick-soled boots, a heavy brace, and padded clothing to make him appear larger and more intimidating. These modifications caused Karloff permanent back pain, making it very difficult for him to walk or even stand up later in his life.

that catapulted Shelley's monster into stardom. Boris Karloff's performance and Jack Pierce's "flat-head" makeup transformed Shelley's monster into the one that most people are familiar with today. Universal Studios made a string of sequels featuring Frankenstein's monster, scaring and entertaining horror fans for more than a decade.

LEAVING THEIR MARK

By the early 1940s, Universal's horror movies were ailing at the box office. Pairing two monsters in a single film, however, proved to be the shot in the arm Universal Studios needed. Despite having a rushed production schedule, the often difficult Lugosi on the set, and a smaller wartime budget, *Frankenstein Meets the Wolf Man* was a big success. These monsters would appear together in several more Universal movies, including *House of Frankenstein* (1944), *House of Dracula* (1945), and the slapstick horror-comedy *Abbott and Costello Meet Frankenstein* (1948). However, they would never regain the popularity achieved in *Frankenstein Meets the Wolf Man*.

CHANEY AND THE WOLF MAN

Of the two stars of the film, Chaney's performance is often looked on as the more original and inspired of the two. With the help of screenwriter Curt Siodmak and makeup artist Jack Pierce, Chaney created one of the most memorable movie roles of all time when he appeared in *The Wolf Man*. Many critics believe his performance in *Frankenstein Meets the Wolf Man* was even better. Much of the film focused on Talbot's struggle against his murderous alter ego, a struggle many critics and fans found engaging, compassionate, and ultimately tragic. For this reason, many fans believe the title of the movie should have been *The Wolf Man Meets Frankenstein*, in honor of Chaney's inspired work.

Many movie critics consider Chaney's best performance to be his role as Lennie in the 1939 film adaptation of the John Steinbeck novel *Of Mice and Men*. However, Chaney is best remembered as the actor who created the modern Wolf Man persona. Chaney himself was frequently quoted as saying that the Wolf Man role was his "baby." Chaney reprised his Talbot/Wolf Man role for *House of Frankenstein*, *House of Dracula*, and *Abbott and Costello Meet Frankenstein*. He continued to act in movies until his death in 1973.

LUGOSI AND FRANKENSTEIN'S MONSTER

Lugosi's performance in *Frankenstein Meets the Wolf Man* is often described as forced and even unintentionally humorous. There are two main reasons for this. In *The Bride of Frankenstein* (1935), the Frankenstein monster developed the ability to speak. In *Frankenstein Meets the Wolf Man*, however, Frankenstein is once again a mute character.

In the original script, the Frankenstein monster had dialogue. However, all of the scenes in which Lugosi had lines were cut shortly after the movie was completed. This was due to the

This is a movie poster for *Abbott and Costello Meet Frankenstein*. Lon Chaney Jr. actually played the role of two monsters in this movie. Besides playing the Wolf Man, he also filled in during one scene for the actor who played Frankenstein's monster (Glenn Strange), who had broken his ankle on the set the day before. Chaney was not working that day, so he stepped into Strange's very large shoes to film the scene as the monster.

negative response Lugosi's speaking scenes received from test audiences. Many people laughed when the monster talked because of Lugosi's thick Hungarian accent, and because of the monster's uncharacteristically intellectual dialogue. Had Lugosi's dialogue been left in, viewers would have realized that

This photo of the cast of *Frankenstein Meets the Wolf Man* shows Lon Chaney Jr. as the Wolf Man, Bela Lugosi as Frankenstein's monster, and Ilona Massey as Elsa Frankenstein. Photos like this were taken before or after filming on the set, and were used for promotional purposes.

Frankenstein's monster—now controlled by the brain of the evil blacksmith Ygor—planned to take over the world!

Frankenstein's monster had become blind in the 1941 movie *The Ghost of Frankenstein*. Lugosi emphasized the monster's blindness by lumbering along with his arms outstretched, as if the monster could not see where he was walking. However, the monster's blindness is not mentioned in *Frankenstein Meets the Wolf Man*. As a result, Lugosi's lumbering walk was ridiculed as overacting. It is interesting to note that Lugosi's performance initiated the stereotypical, stiff-legged walk most people associate with Frankenstein's monster.

Most critics agree that Lugosi's best role was his portrayal of the vampire in the 1931 film *Dracula*. He appeared as Count Dracula one last time in *Abbott and Costello Meet Frankenstein*, which was his last Universal Studios picture. After that, Lugosi was cast in numerous horror films, but he never regained the superstar status he had in the 1930s. Lugosi's health declined rapidly through the 1940s, in part because of an addiction to morphine, which he had originally begun taking to relieve severe back pain. On August 16, 1956, Lugosi died of a drug-related heart attack. Following his own request, Lugosi was buried wearing his full Dracula costume.

THE LEGACY OF FRANKENSTEIN AND THE WOLF MAN

Other monster rallies followed *Frankenstein Meets the Wolf Man*, but none were as successful. By the mid-1950s, Universal monster movies were a thing of the past, and new horrors began to take their place. Color film, improved cameras, dazzling special effects, and better makeup techniques quickly changed the horror movie genre. Frankenstein's monster and the Wolf Man were brushed aside for newer monsters. This is not to say, however, that these classic monsters were forgotten.

PAYING HOMAGE TO UNIVERSAL'S HORROR MOVIES

In 1974, director Mel Brooks and actor Gene Wilder wrote and filmed *Young Frankenstein*. Wilder and Brooks created this parody as a tribute to Universal's horror films of the 1930s and 1940s—specifically the *Frankenstein* series. Not only was the film shot in black and white to capture the feel of the 1931 *Frankenstein*, it was filmed in the same castle with the same props and laboratory equipment. This movie is filled with references to Universal's *Frankenstein* movies, playfully making fun of and honoring the series at the same time.

Pictured here is the main cast of *Young Frankenstein* (1974). From left to right are the beautiful lab assistant, Inga (Teri Garr), Dr. Frederick Frankenstein (Gene Wilder), Igor the hunchbacked lab assistant (Marty Feldman), and, in front of this trio, the monster (Peter Boyle). To the right is director Mel Brooks, who does not appear in the movie.

WEREWOLVES OF THE 1980S

By the early 1980s, new special-effects techniques allowed filmmakers to do things that had never been done before. *The Howling* (1980), directed by Joe Dante, pays homage to the directors of werewolf movies by naming the characters after them. In fact, much of *The Howling* is filled with jokes that only the most rabid werewolf fans would recognize. A year later, *An American Werewolf in London* was released. Written and directed by John Landis, *An American Werewolf in London* is both scary and funny.

Both movies used similar special effects to show werewolf transformations in slow, graphic, terrifying detail. Special- effects artists and makeup experts Rick Baker and Rob Bottin created realistic-looking puppets and prosthetic limbs filled with air bladders, or balloons. These bladders were slowly filled with air, causing the puppets to stretch, grow fangs, and sprout hair. This method helped to create the most realistic and gruesome werewolf transformations to date.

FRANKENSTEIN RETURNS

Thanks to Universal's catalog of *Frankenstein* movies—as well as the many other versions of the story that have been released since the 1940s—the Frankenstein's monster most people are familiar with differs greatly from the monster of Mary Shelley's novel. In 1994, Kenneth Branagh directed and starred in *Mary Shelley's Frankenstein*, which is the most literal screen adaptation of Shelley's story to date. While the movie differs in some ways from Shelley's story, Branagh's movie follows the same basic plot and contains the same basic ideas, most of which have been omitted from modern adaptations of Shelley's novel. Frankenstein's monster, played by Robert De Niro, is not the flat-headed, hulking, growling monster of Universal's movies. Rather, it is an intelligent, passionate creation capable of a broad range of human emotions, as Shelley herself had intended it to be.

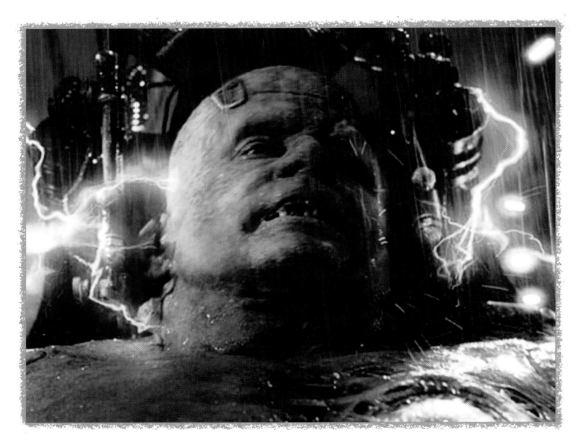

Van Helsing (2004) was the first movie to feature the Wolf Man, Frankenstein's monster, and Dracula in the same movie since *Abbott and Costello Meet Frankenstein*. In this still from the movie, Frankenstein's monster (Shuler Hensley) receives a blast of electricity. Despite the use of modern special effects and makeup techniques, it still took about 4.5 hours to apply Hensley's monster makeup, and about an hour to remove it.

THE NEW MONSTER RALLY

Frankenstein's monster, the Wolf Man, and Dracula were united once again in 2004 for the movie *Van Helsing*. Hugh Jackman plays a notorious monster hunter in this thrilling and often humorous horror movie. Cutting-edge computer graphics were used to create terrifying monsters and stunning action scenes, breathing new life into three of the horror movie industry's most recognizable monsters.

STAMP OF APPROVAL

Universal Studios' movie monsters have had a long-lasting effect on popular culture. In 1997, the U.S. Postal Service honored four Universal horror movie actors by releasing the Classic Movie Monsters postage stamps. Indirectly, these stamps also commemorate the work of makeup artist Jack Pierce, who helped to elevate each of the actors to superstar status. These stamps feature five classic Universal monsters: the Phantom of the Opera (Lon Chaney), Dracula (Bela Lugosi), Frankenstein's monster (Boris Karloff), the Mummy (Karloff), and the Wolf Man (Lon Chaney Jr.). Without horror movie pioneers such as Lon Chaney Jr. and Bela Lugosi, the Wolf Man and Frankenstein's monster would not be as popular as they are today.

FILMOGRAPHY

Frankenstein (1931) Universal Studios' blockbuster transformed Mary Shelley's original creation into the creature that most people are familiar with today. Horror heavy hitter Boris Karloff stars as the monster.

Bride of Frankenstein (1935) A mad scientist kidnaps Dr. Frankenstein's wife and forces Dr. Frankenstein to make another creature—a bride for his notorious monster. Karloff returns as the monster.

The Son of Frankenstein (1939) The son of Dr. Frankenstein, Wolf, returns to his father's castle to claim his inheritance. A blacksmith named Ygor forces Wolf to revive the monster from his coma so he can use it for evil purposes. Karloff once again plays the monster, and Bela Lugosi plays Ygor.

The Wolf Man (1941) Lawrence Talbot (Lon Chaney Jr.) kills a werewolf (Bela Lugosi), but he is bitten during the fight. As a result, Talbot also becomes a werewolf.

The Ghost of Frankenstein (1942) Ygor (again played by Lugosi) saves the monster and brings it to another of Dr. Frankenstein's sons—Ludwig. With evil thoughts of domination, Ygor tricks Ludwig into transplanting his own brain into the monster. Lon Chaney Jr. plays the monster.

House of Frankenstein (1944) An evil scientist (Boris Karloff) revives Dracula, Frankenstein's monster, and the Wolf Man for the purpose of getting revenge against his enemies.

Chaney returns as the Wolf Man in the second of Universal Studios' monster rallies.

House of Dracula (1945) All three monsters—Dracula, Frankenstein, and the Wolf Man—return once again in Universal Studios' third monster rally. Chaney once again plays the Wolf Man.

Abbott and Costello Meet Frankenstein (1948) In the last of the rally movies, humor joins forces with horror. Dracula tries to steal the brain of a bumbling freight handler and use it to turn Frankenstein's monster into his mindless henchman. Lawrence Talbot arrives in search of Dracula. Lugosi returns as Dracula, and Chaney once again plays the Wolf Man.

Young Frankenstein (1974) Directed by Mel Brooks and shot in black and white, this horror-comedy is both a spoof of and a tribute to Universal's horror movies of the 1930s and 1940s. Gene Wilder plays Dr. Frederick Frankenstein and Peter Boyle plays the monster.

The Howling (1980) A newswoman goes to a retreat on the California coast with her husband after being attacked by a serial killer. The members of the retreat turn out to be a pack of werewolves. Along with *An American Werewolf in London*, this film is well known as one of the first movies to show a graphic werewolf transformation.

An American Werewolf in London (1981) In this horror-comedy, two Americans are attacked by werewolves while hiking in Europe. One man is killed but returns from the dead to warn his friend that he will soon turn into a werewolf. Rick Baker won the first-ever Oscar for Best Makeup for his work on this movie.

Mary Shelley's Frankenstein (1994) The closest film adaptation of Shelley's original story. Kenneth Branagh directs and stars as Victor Frankenstein, and Robert De Niro plays the monster.

Van Helsing (2004) Monster hunter Dr. Gabriel Van Helsing (Hugh Jackman) battles Dracula, Frankenstein's monster, and the Wolf Man. Computer-generated special effects breathe new life into these classic horror icons.

GLOSSARY

alter ego A second or contrary personality.

articulate Capable of clear and effective expression.

cliché A convention that has become expected or even boring from overuse.

conceited Having an exaggerated sense of self-importance.

gothic novel A genre of fiction that originated in the mid-1700s. Gothic novels commonly dealt with dark themes, spooky settings, and supernatural developments.

immortality Unending life.

parody A creative work that imitates another work for the purpose of creating a comedic effect.

pentagram A five-pointed star drawn with a continuous line. Often used as a magic or occult symbol.

prosthetic An artificial device designed to replace or resemble a part of the human body.

romantic period An intellectual movement that originated in the eighteenth century in western Europe. The romantic period was marked by strong emotions, imaginative thought, and a turning away from social conventions.

test audience A group of people to whom a movie is shown before it is released in theaters for the purpose of gauging public reaction.

transformation The act or process of changing.

FOR MORE INFORMATION

American Film Institute
2021 N. Western Avenue
Los Angeles, CA 90027-1657
(323) 856-7600
Web Site: http://www.afi.com

Universal Studios
100 Universal City Plaza
Universal City, CA 91608
(818) 508-9600
Web Site: http://www.universalstudios.com

WEB SITES

Due to the changing nature of Internet links, the Rosen Publishing Group, Inc., has developed an online list of Web sites related to the subject of this book. This site is updated regularly. Please use this link to access the list:

http://www.rosenlinks.com/famm/frmw

FOR FURTHER READING

Jacobs, David. *The Devil's Night: The New Adventures of Dracula, Frankenstein & the Universal Monsters*. Berkeley, CA: Berkeley Publishing Group, 2001.

Powel, Eric, et al. *Universal Monsters: Cavalcade of Horror.* Milwaukie, OR: Dark Horse Comics, 2006.

Renfield, R. K. *Meet the Wolf Man*. New York, NY: The Rosen Publishing Group, Inc., 2005.

Shelley, Mary. *Frankenstein*. New York, NY: Pocket Books, 2004.

Soister, John T. *Of Gods and Monsters: A Critical Guide to Universal Studios' Science Fiction, Horror, and Mystery Films, 1929–1939*. Jefferson, NC: McFarland & Company, 2005.

Youngson, Jeanne Keyes. *The Encyclopedia of Vampires, Werewolves, and Other Monsters*. New York, NY: Checkmark Books, 2004.

BIBLIOGRAPHY

Berardinelli, James. "Mary Shelley's Frankenstein." ReelViews. 1994. Retrieved November 2005 (http://movie-reviews. colossus.net/movies/m/mary_shellys.html).

"Biography for Bela Lugosi." IMDb (Internet Movie Database). Retrieved November 2005 (http://www.imdb.com/name/ nm0000509/bio).

"Biography for Jack P. Pierce." IMDb (Internet Movie Database). Retrieved November 2005 (http://www.imdb.com/name/ nm0682370/bio).

"Biography for John P. Fulton." IMDb (Internet Movie Database). Retrieved November 2005 (http://www.imdb.com/name/ nm0298483/bio).

"Biography for Lon Chaney Jr." IMDb (Internet Movie Database). Retrieved November 2005 (http://www.imdb.com/name/ nm0001033/bi).

Blessings, Mary, and Timothy R. Carnahan, translator. "The Epic of Gilgamesh." Academy for Ancient Texts. June 7, 2001. Retrieved November 2005 (http://www.ancienttexts.org/ library/mesopotamian/gilgamesh).

Brunas, Michael, et al. *Universal Horrors: The Studio's Classic Films, 1931–1946*. Jefferson, NC: McFarland & Company, Inc., 1990.

Copper, Basil. *The Werewolf in Legend, Fact and Art*. New York, NY: St. Martin's Press, 1977.

Cybulski, Angela. *Werewolves: Fact or Fiction?* Farmington Hills, MI: Greenhaven Press, 2004.

"Frankenstein." Wikipedia. Retrieved November 2005 (http://en.wikipedia.org/wiki/Frankenstein).

Garden, Nancy. *Werewolves.* New York, NY: J. B. Lippincott Company, 1973.

Glut, Donald F. *Classic Movie Monsters.* Metuchen, NJ: The Scarecrow Press, Inc., 1978.

Glut, Donald F. *The Frankenstein Archive: Essays on the Monster, the Myth, the Movies, and More.* Jefferson, NC: McFarland, 2002.

"Jack Pierce." Wikipedia. Retrieved November 2005 (http://en.wikipedia.org/wiki/Jack_Pierce).

Lenning, Arthur. *The Immortal Count: The Life and Films of Bela Lugosi.* Lexington, KY: The University Press of Kentucky, 2003.

"Lycaon." Encycloaedia Britannica. 2005. Retrieved November 2005 (http://www.britannica.com/eb/article-9049479).

Mitchell, Stephen. *Gilgamesh: A New English Version.* New York, NY: Free Press, 2004.

Nardo, Don. *Understanding Frankenstein.* Farmington Hills, MI: Lucent Books, 2003.

Picart, Caroline Joan S., et al. *The Frankenstein Film Sourcebook.* Westport, CT: Greenwood Press, 2001.

Scheib, Richard. "Frankenstein Meets the Wolf Man." The Science Fiction, Horror and Fantasy Film Review. 2000. Retrieved November 2005 (http://www.moria.co.nz/horror/frmeetswolfman.htm).

"Universal Horror." Wikipedia. Retrieved November 2005 (http://en.wikipedia.org/wiki/Universal_Horror).

"Werewolf." Wikipedia. Retrieved November 2005
(http://en.wikipedia.org/wiki/Werewolf).

"The Wolf Man." Wikipedia. Retrieved November 2005
(http://en.wikipedia.org/wiki/Wolf_Man).

INDEX

ABOUT THE AUTHOR

Greg Roza lives in Hamburg, New York, with his wife, Abigail, his daughter, Autumn, and his son, Lincoln. Roza has a masters degree in English from SUNY Fredonia and is a writer and editor of children's books. Ever since his early childhood, Roza has had a fondness for horror movies, especially the classics.

PHOTO CREDITS

Cover, pp. 1, 4, 11, 20, 29 © Photofest; p. 5 © Underwood & Underwood/ Corbis; pp. 8, 10, 13, 18, 24, 31, 32 Everett Collection; pp. 12, 15, 21, 25, 28 © Bettmann/Corbis; p. 16 © John Springer Collection/Corbis; p. 23 © Bildarchiv Preussischer Kulturebesitz/Art Resource, NY; p. 34 © 20th Century Fox Film Corp. All Rights reserved. Courtesy Everett Collection; p. 36 © Universal/Courtesy Everett Collection.

Designer: Thomas Forget